CALUMET CITY PUBLIC LIBRARY

3 1613 00443 2079

P9-BYD-977

J
741.5
JON

Learn to Draw Manga

MANGA SUPERHEROES

Illustrated by
Richard Jones & Jorge Santillan

PowerKiDS
press
New York

CALUMET CITY PUBLIC LIBRARY

Published in 2013 by The Rosen Publishing Group, Inc.
29 East 21st Street, New York, NY 10010

Copyright © 2013 by The Rosen Publishing Group, Inc.

All rights reserved. No part of this book may be reproduced in any form without permission in writing from the publisher, except by a reviewer.

First Edition

Produced for Rosen by Calcium Creative Ltd
Editor: Sarah Eason
Editor for Rosen: Sara Antill
Book Design: Paul Myerscough

Illustrations by Richard Jones and Jorge Santillan

Library of Congress Cataloging-in-Publication Data

Jones, Richard.
Manga superheroes / by Richard Jones & Jorge Santillan. — 1st ed.
    p. cm. — (Learn to draw manga)
Includes index.
ISBN 978-1-4488-7877-2 (library binding) —
ISBN 978-1-4488-7948-9 (pbk.) — ISBN 978-1-4488-7954-0 (6-pack)
1. Superheroes in art—Juvenile literature. 2. Comic strip characters—
Juvenile literature. 3. Comic books, strips, etc.—Japan--Technique—
Juvenile literature. 4. Cartooning—Technique—Juvenile literature.
I. Santillan, Jorge. II. Title.
NC1764.8.H47J66 2013
741.5'1—dc23

2011053449

Manufactured in the United States of America

CPSIA Compliance Information: Batch #B4S12PK: For Further Information contact Rosen Publishing, New York, New York at 1-800-237-9932

Contents

"Manga" is a Japanese word that means "comic." Manga superheroes are some of the most exciting cartoon characters you'll ever see, and now you can learn to draw incredible Manga heroes yourself!

Manga gets heroic

In this book, we are going to show you how to draw some superheroes with the most amazing powers, Manga-style!

You will need

To create your Manga superheroes, you will need some equipment:

Sketchpad or paper
Try to use good quality paper from an art store.

Pencils
A set of good drawing pencils are key to creating great character drawings.

Eraser
Use this to remove any unwanted lines.

Paintbrush, paints, and pens
The final stage for all your drawings will be to add color. We have used paints to complete the Manga characters in this book. If you prefer, you could use pens.

Elf Girl Archer

Energy charges through this heroine's bow and arrow, and her aim is electric!

Step 1

Draw the outline for your heroine's body. Exaggerate the size of her left hand, so it appears to be close to you.

Step 2

Add the bow, arrow, and the arrow holder. Draw the features on the face, the hair, and the outfit.

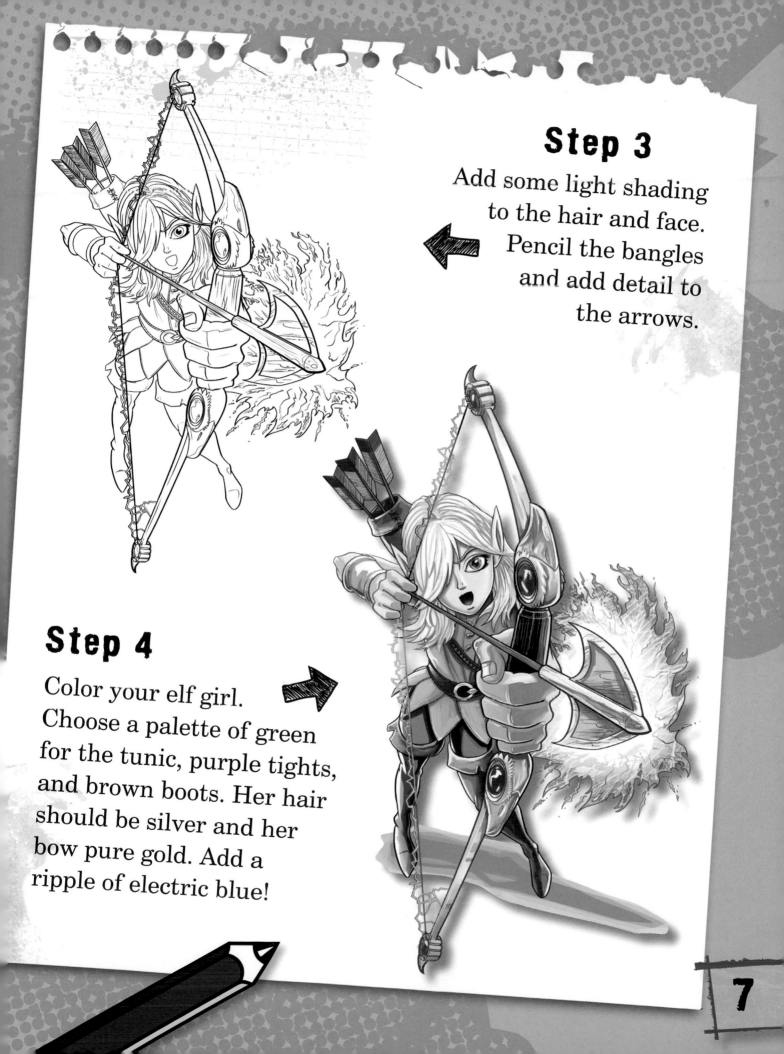

Step 3

Add some light shading to the hair and face. Pencil the bangles and add detail to the arrows.

Step 4

Color your elf girl. Choose a palette of green for the tunic, purple tights, and brown boots. Her hair should be silver and her bow pure gold. Add a ripple of electric blue!

Laserbeam Superhero

Red-hot laserbeams dart from this superhero's eyes, burning through anything in their path!

Step 1

Draw your superhero in a lunging pose, with one hand raised to the side of his head. Use cone shapes for the legs and arms and a circular shape for the head. Draw two lines for the laserbeam.

Step 2

Add muscle detail to the chest and arms. Roughly pencil the eyes.

Step 3

Now add a shock of ragged hair, the boots, shoulder pads, and belt. Pencil the bands on the arms. Draw the flash of the laserbeam.

Step 4

Erase any unwanted, rough lines and add some shading to the face.

Sharpen your skills

Try a different pose in which your hero is running with one leg raised behind him.

Step 5

Paint the bodysuit a light blue. Add flashes of green on the pants, boots, shoulder pads, and arm bands. Paint touches of orange. Finish with brown hair, a bright red laserbeam, and white highlights.

Flying Fighter

Flying faster than the speed of sound, this Manga warrior is on a rescue mission!

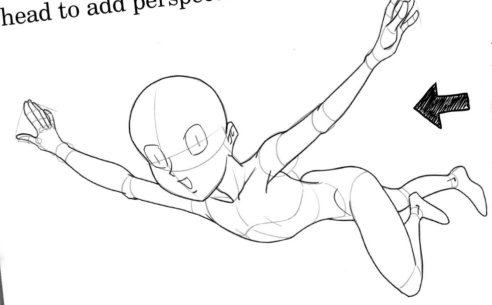

Step 1

Draw your character with arms stretched out and one leg curled beneath. Exaggerate the size of the head to add perspective.

Step 2

Add the eyes, nose, ear, and mouth. Pencil detail on the fingers.

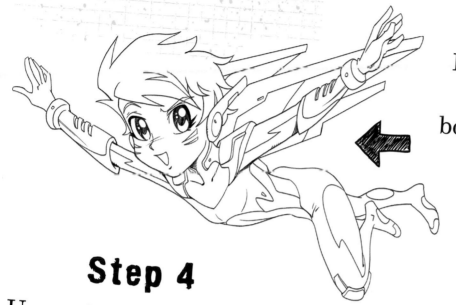

Step 3

Draw the heroine's hair, wings, and bodysuit. Add detail to the arm bands and shading to the eyes.

Step 4

Use a strong, bright blue for the warrior's hair. Color the clothing with a pink and purple palette. Add blue lines to show her supersonic speed!

Jetpack Superhero

Manga superheroes have super powers. Some have the strength of a giant, while others have the speed of a lightning bolt! A supersonic jetpack powers this fearless fighter.

Step 1

Draw circles and cone shapes to create a rough structure for your jetpack fighter.

Step 2

Draw a line from the top of the head to the end of the torso. Carefully mark the muscles of the body. Draw the fingers, toes, and ears.

Step 3

Using light pencil strokes, add the rough detailed lines. Draw in the hair, face, clothing, and the arm guns. Pencil in the jetpack and wings.

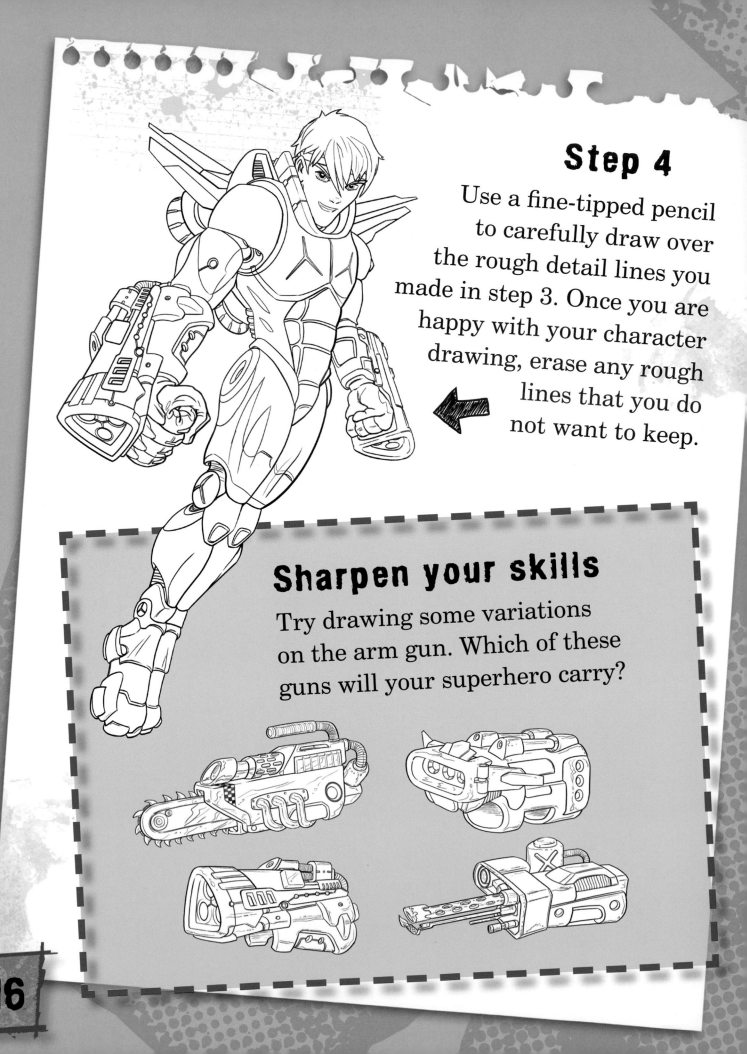

Step 4

Use a fine-tipped pencil to carefully draw over the rough detail lines you made in step 3. Once you are happy with your character drawing, erase any rough lines that you do not want to keep.

Sharpen your skills

Try drawing some variations on the arm gun. Which of these guns will your superhero carry?

Step 5

Now it's time to color your jetpack hero. Use a bright purple paint for the body suit, with patches of light gray for the detailed areas. Add flashes of orange, yellow, and red markings on the clothing. Finally, give your superhero bright blue eyes and a head of blue hair.

CALUMET CITY PUBLIC LIBRARY

3 1613 00443 2079

Bionic Boy Runner

Moving faster than the speed of light, a bionic body gives this character superhuman speed.

Step 1

Draw your character in a running pose, head down and arm reaching forward. One leg is raised behind. Add muscle lines to the bionic body.

Step 2

Pencil the hair and the detail of the face. Half of the face is made of bionic material, as shown opposite.

Step 3

Use a fine-tipped pencil to add the clothing, with torn sections that reveal bionic muscles.

Step 4

Choose a silver paint for the bionic body, with blue and white highlights. Give your bionic boy flaming orange hair!

Muscle Man

This muscle-packed hulk is incredibly strong. Only the bravest fighter would dare to challenge him!

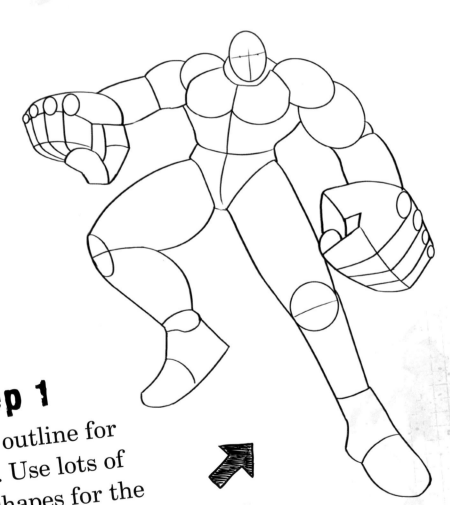

Step 1

Pencil the outline for your hero. Use lots of rounded shapes for the muscles and large cone shapes for the legs. Draw enormous hands.

Step 2

Add further detail to the muscles with a "six pack" on the stomach and lines to show the thigh and arm muscles.

Step 3

Give your mega fighter spiky hair and pencil the detail of the boots, knee pads, and thigh straps. Add the branch that the muscle man has broken in two!

21

Step 4

Use a fine-tipped pencil to add depth. Shade the muscle lines and the thigh straps. Add shading to the hair and branch.

Sharpen your skills

If you want your muscle man to be really mad, draw him holding a car above his head!

Step 5

Now it's time to bring your character to life.
Give him bright, red hair and a green body
suit. Use a darker green for the straps and
knee pads. The branch could be a dark red.
Show off those muscles with white highlights!

Fireball Master

This fire-throwing villain flies through the sky on his magic carpet, destroying anything in his path. The heat of a fireball is his weapon.

Step 1

Draw your antihero in a stooped position, leaning forward to release the flames from his hands.

Step 2

Pencil the detail to the edges of the flames and erase the rough outline. Add the muscle details to the body and the features of the face.

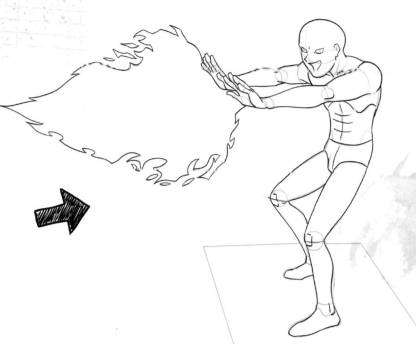

Step 3

Draw the clothing, hair, and boots. Add stud details to the arms of the jacket and the pants. Add more flames.

Step 4

Use a fine-tipped pencil to add lots of detailed shading to the boots and clothing.

Sharpen your skills

This super villain is so powerful, he can throw flames from just one hand! Try out this pose, too.

Step 5

Your evil-looking character has a mane of thick red hair. Color his pants purple, with gray studs. Use a dark gray for the arm shields and the jacket. Color the flame yellow and orange, with some white highlights. Don't forget to color the skyrider's magical carpet in blues and greens.

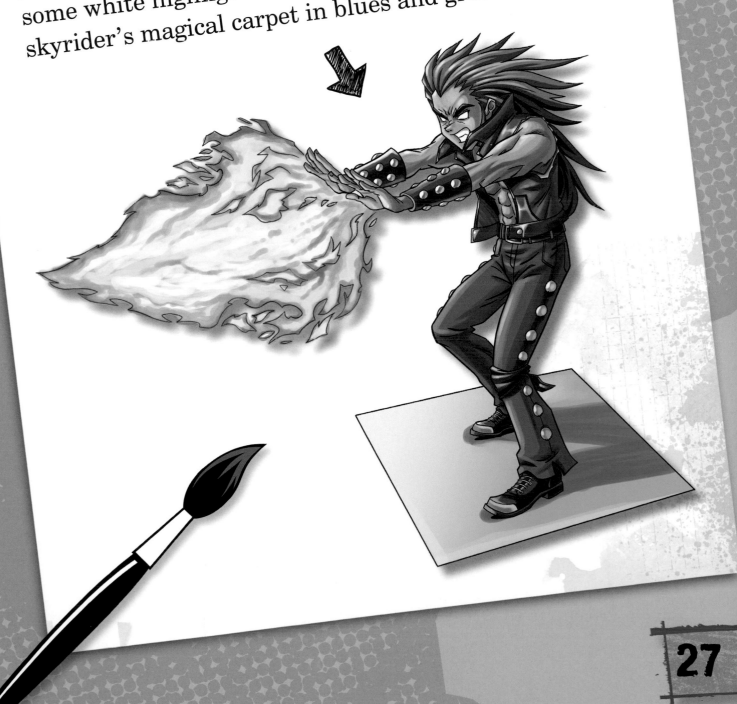

More Heroes

If you've loved drawing Manga superheroes, try some more!

Lightning Thrower

Bolts of lightning blast from this boy hero!

Sky Pirate

Archenemy of any Manga superhero, this sky pirate is a freakish fiend!

Samurai Girl

With her deadly samurai sword, this fighter girl is a fierce warrior.

Elf Boy Warrior

The elf girl archer's twin brother fights with an unbreakable magic wand.

Glossary

antihero (AN-tee-heer-oh) A villain, opposite of a hero.

archer (AR-chur) A person who uses a bow and arrow.

character (KER-ik-tur) A fictional, or made-up person. Can also mean the features that you recognize something or someone by.

deadly (DED-lee) Can kill.

detail (dih-TAYL) The smaller, finer lines that are used to add important features to a character drawing, such as eyes, ears, and hair.

erase (ih-RAYS) To remove.

exaggerate (eg-ZA-juh-rayt) To make bigger than it really is.

fine-tipped (fyn-TIHPD) A sharp tip of a pencil or pen.

highlights (HY-lytz) Light parts.

laserbeams (LAY-zer-beemz) Beams of extremely hot light.

lunging (LUN-jing) Moving suddenly forward.

outline (OWT-lyn) A very simple line that provides the shape for a drawing.

palette (PA-lit) A range of colors.

perspective (per-SPEK-tiv) A sense of distance.

pose (POHZ) The way something or somebody stands.

ragged (RA-ged) Having a rough edge.

samurai (SA-muh-ry) A Japanese warrior.

shading (SHAYD-ing) Creating lots of soft, heavy lines to add shadow and depth to a drawing.

supersonic (soo-per-SAH-nik) Faster than the speed of sound.

tunic (TOO-nik) A very short coatlike piece of clothing.

villain (VI-len) A bad person.

Cook, Trevor, and Lisa Miles. *Drawing Manga. Drawing Is Fun.* New York: Gareth Stevens, 2011.

Hansen, Jim, and John Burns. *Creating Manga Superheroes and Comic Book Characters.* New York: Gramercy Books, 2006.

Okum, David. *Superhero Madness.* Cincinnati, OH: Impact Books, 2004.

Southgate, Anna, and Keith Sparrow. *Drawing Manga Expressions and Poses. Manga Magic.* New York: Rosen Publishing, 2012.

Due to the changing nature of Internet links, PowerKids Press has developed an online list of websites related to the subject of this book. This site is updated regularly. Please use this link to access the list: www.powerkidslinks.com/ltdm/hero/

Websites

Index